Cartoons to cheer up a
GRUMPY OLD GIT

by The Odd Squad

CARTOONS TO CHEER UP A GRUMPY OLD GIT

© 2011 by Allan Penderleith

All rights reserved

First published in 2011 by
Ravette Publishing Limited
PO Box 876, Horsham, West Sussex RH12 9GH

ISBN: 978-1-84161-360-4

The new website for old gits.

When kissing a woman,
try not to burp.

Jeff had a feeling Billy was spending too much time on the Xbox.

Never ask a man to change the baby.

Never drink and drive.

Dave spent the weekend camping.

WOOF!

How to make a cat go woof.

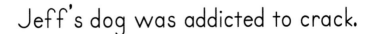

Jeff hates chick flicks.

The new Yorkshire-based
auction site: E-bay Gum.

Jeff hates his eggs runny.

His mate always knew what Dug was
getting for his birthday.

Jeff is caught fly-tipping.

Jeff's plans had gone to pot.

Jeff couldn't help staring
at his wife's great rack.

Dug spent the weekend
hanging with his homies.

As Jeff entered the remote country pub,
he realised the locals were in-bread.

Dug regretted getting a job at
the kebab factory.

Jeff had actually asked the waiter
to make his curry a little hotter.

Man boobs.

Jeff regretted putting roaming on his mobile.

Jeff bought a large memory stick.

Whilst surfing the net at work,
Jeff got an embarrassing pop-up.

Once again, Jeff had put too much helium in the party balloons.

Jeff noticed a ring of
scum around the bath.

Whilst installing a new computer programme, Jeff had trouble with the setup wizard.

Billy had been watching
too much Top Gear.

Jeff had to use the loo fast,
he had the turtle's head.

Suddenly Jeff wished he hadn't changed his desktop wallpaper.

Jeff woke up with a disgusting
film on his teeth.

As Jeff cycled up the hill he realised he was in the wrong gear.

Jeff's computer was
low on cache.

Jeff had actually ordered
aromatic duck.

Jeff tests the smoke alarm.

Other ODD SQUAD gift books available ...

	ISBN	PRICE
Cartoons to Cheer up a Stroppy Mare	978-1-84161-361-1	£4.99
I Love Beer	978-1-84161-238-6	£5.99
I Love Dad	978-1-84161-252-2	£5.99
I Love Mum	978-1-84161-249-2	£5.99
I Love Poo	978-1-84161-240-9	£5.99
I Love Sex	978-1-84161-241-6	£4.99
I Love Wine	978-1-84161-239-3	£4.99
I Love Xmas	978-1-84161-262-1	£4.99
Little Book of Booze	978-1-84161-138-9	£2.99
Little Book of Men	978-1-84161-093-1	£2.99
Little Book of Pumping	978-1-84161-140-2	£2.50
Little Book of Sex	978-1-84161-095-5	£2.99
Little Book of X-rated Cartoons	978-1-84161-141-9	£2.99

HOW TO ORDER:

Please send a cheque/postal order in £ sterling, made payable to 'Ravette Publishing' for the cover price of the book/s and allow the following for post & packing ...

UK & BFPO	70p for the first book & 40p per book thereafter
Europe & Eire	£1.30 for the first book & 70p per book thereafter
Rest of the world	£2.20 for the first book & £1.10 per book thereafter

RAVETTE PUBLISHING LTD
PO Box 876, Horsham, West Sussex RH12 9GH
Tel: 01403 711443 Fax: 01403 711554 Email: ingrid@ravettepub.co.uk

Prices and availability are subject to change without prior notice